Beautiful
Idaho

Beautiful
Idaho

Text by Paul M. Lewis

Library of Congress Cataloging in Publication Data
Lewis, Paul M.
 Beautiful Idaho
 1. Idaho—Description and travel—1951-
I. Title.
F747.B4   917.96'02   79-779
ISBN 0-915796-93-7
ISBN 0-915796-92-9 (paperback)

First Printing June 1979

Published by Beautiful America Publishing Company
4720 S.W. Washington, Beaverton, Oregon 97005
Robert D. Shangle, Publisher

Copyright © 1979 by Beautiful America Publishing Company
Printed in the United States of America

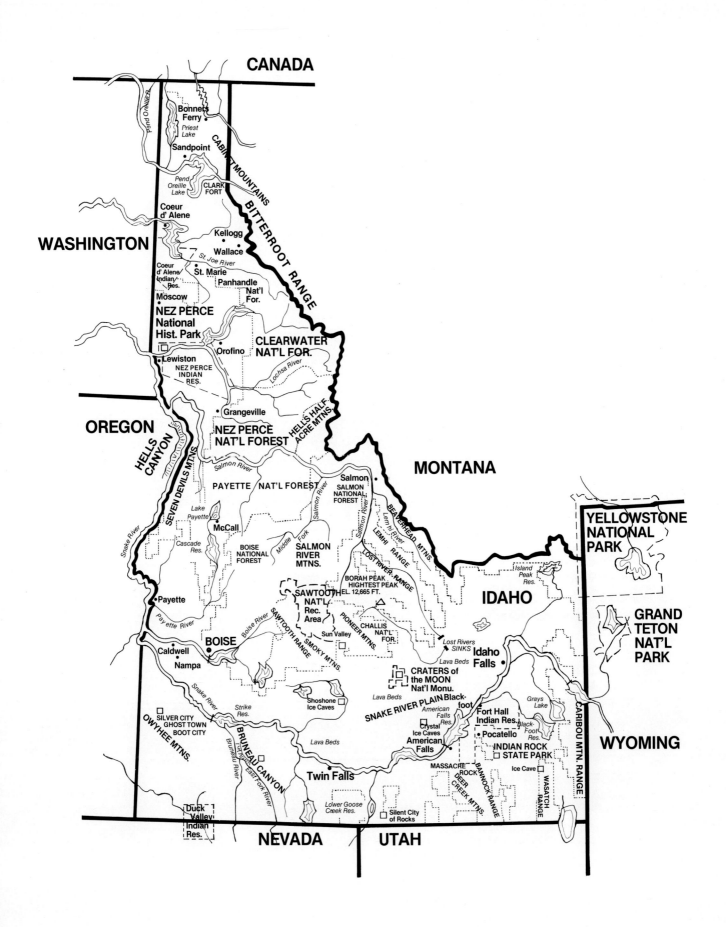

CONTENTS

Introduction 6

The Panhandle 8

Northern and Central Idaho 30

The Kingdom of the Snake 58

PHOTO CREDITS

ROY BISHOP—*page 43, below.*
BOB CLEMENZ—*pages 12-13; pages 16-17; page 28; pages 44-45; page 46.*
ED COOPER—*page 11, below; page 18, below; page 37; page 47, below; page 52; page 53, above; page 56, below; page 68.*
DUANE DAVIS—*page 9; page 21, below; page 24, below; page 29, below; page 41; page 57; pages 64-65; page 72.*
ROSS HALL—*page 47, above.*
JOHN HILL—*page 23, below; page 60.*
TOM JONES—*page 15; page 18, above; page 24, above; page 29, above.*
STEVE & CANDY MOEN, and CHRIS KROMM—*page 19; page 69.*
PAT O'HARA—*page 14; pages 32-33; pages 48-49; page 61.*
ROBERT SHANGLE—*page 21, above; page 23, above; page 50, above; page 55, above; page 55, below.*
DAVID SUMNER—*page 20; page 22; page 25; page 36; page 40, above; page 43, above; page 50, below; page 51; page 54.*
BRUCE and SAM WHITE—*page 10; page 11, above; page 40, below; page 42; page 53, below; page 56, above.*

THE INDESCRIBABLE STATE

A curious feature of humankind is the tendency, nay, the compulsion, of the individual to regard his dwelling place as superior to any other on earth. Maybe other forms of animal life are programmed this way too; it's hard to tell, given the tentative nature of our communications with different species. Until someone does some definitive research on this important matter, all we can say for certain is that almost any human being will brag about the place he lives without even being asked.

The United States is gifted with all kinds of beautiful and wonderful scenic features. And it has raised a bumper crop of braggarts, who identify with some part of that natural beauty and even feel a kind of ownership of it. Even Idahoans indulge in this custom. But being less than one-twentieth the number of, say, 20 million Californians, or merely one-tenth the teeming multitudes who admit to being Floridians, the resulting promotional thunder is a comparatively faint rumble.

There is no one way to describe Idaho, so it's sometimes difficult to get an "accurate" picture of the place. Its range of contrasts may surpass that of any other part of the United States. The mountain, lake, and forest regimes of the Panhandle and central Idaho are light-years removed in form and feeling from the dry plateaus and eroded canyons of the Owyhee country in the southwest or the bleak and barren steppes of the Snake River Plain, reaching in a broad band across southern Idaho. On the other hand, near the great river around Pocatello and Blackfoot and Idaho Falls are huge, green irrigated areas of sugar beets, peas, and famous Idaho spuds.

Idaho is plumbed as is no other state. It has the most running and falling water, much of it originating in the dense forests of remote mountain wilderness. The swift, flashing streams of Idaho are almost beyond counting—the Salmon, Clearwater, Priest, Selway, Lochsa, and parts of the great Snake itself, are among the bigger ones. There's even a prominent exception to the quick-time pace of the majority. That's the placid St. Joe, which pokes along a leisurely 72-mile course to Lake Coeur d'Alene.

In constrast with the rivers, Idaho is also a land of sand dunes and sagebrush plains where trees are nonexistent and water is hard to come by except at the bottom of a canyon. Parts of it are very cold at times, and parts of it, very hot. Certain localities like the low-level Lewiston area usually avoid either extreme. So it's hard, even for an Idahoan, to say what Idaho is like. It's more like a nation than a state, with a reach north to the Canadian border and south to Nevada and Utah. Its kaleidoscopic range of spectacle stretches the meaning of the word "variety."

Idaho is still one of those states where people are relatively scarce. Being a human being myself, I'm all for them—but not in large numbers. Where humanity gathers in its multitudes it manages to de-naturalize the living space in its search for living space.

Most of Idaho has so far escaped being remodeled in man's image. From the point of view of this book that is a good thing, because our purpose has been to reproduce in dazzling photographs and, I hope, evocative prose, the essence of Idaho in all, or most, of its *natural* glory. No improvements can be made upon it, and we can only hope that for a very long time none will be attempted. The Idaho idyll can only be endangered by audacious "development" of its priceless natural and scenic resources.

But I don't think that will happen. Some rearranging here and there has been necessary so that people can wrest a livelihood from the earth and otherwise have the things that we've grown accustomed to having. There are those dams on the Snake and on some of its tributaries, but the extent of their impact has so far been confined to relatively small areas. Inevitably, as more and more people discover the Gem State, its wilderness will come under increasing pressure. Maybe, before things get out of hand, Idaho should consider locking its borders and henceforth letting people in only at the replacement level.

P.M.L.

THE PANHANDLE

It is green and mountainous and watery, and considering its northerly latitudes, quite mild. The Idaho Panhandle is a gentle wilderness, very different from the big bulge of the state to the south. It is exceptionally well-endowed with clear, pure water. Its lakes are super-beautiful; many miles of their shorelines and beaches have that look of new discovery, of not yet having felt the vacationers' sometimes heavy tread.

The remote look may be only an illusion. During the travel season people suddenly remember there is an Idaho, and its Panhandle is a favorite destination for vacations with a built-in tranquilizer. Eastern Washingtonians, especially, seem to find the Panhandle country irresistible.

To say there are lakes everywhere in this narrow corridor is hardly an exaggeration. Hundreds of small lakes lie unheralded in mountain valleys and at lower elevations. Many an Idahoan who lives in these parts would just as soon keep it that way—he has his favorite little watery jewel off the tourist track, a special place reserved for him and maybe a few other home folks. The maze of rivers and lakes makes it easy to understand why the Panhandle spawned the "Gem State" sobriquet. And these waterways have been useful as well as beautiful. Some of the biggest gold strikes of the frenzied end-of-the-century mining period were made in the Panhandle. (Today, most of our silver comes from here). The miners used the waterways for transportation, and in this century loggers float their logs down the same natural carriers. Other men in other carriers—settlers, prospectors, missionaries—have also traveled the waters of northern Idaho.

Lake Coeur d'Alene became a busy setting for the mournful and musical wail of steamboat whistles during the developing period of the Northwest. The steamboats carried everything that was necessary to keep the youthful territory's growing-up spasms supplied with fuel: gold, silver, and lead; lumber, cattle, produce; river fish; mail from the distant East; and people. In the later Coeur d'Alene steamboat era—well into this century—excursions between various lake towns and trips on the St. Joe and St. Maries rivers became big business.

Although the steamboats have disappeared, Lake Coeur d'Alene has not. Pleasure craft and houseboats are now the *modus* for those who want to get close to its deep blue surface and explore its enchanting, forested bays. With no more effort than it takes to look through a car window, the highway traveler can have an ever-changing perspective of the lake by driving along a road that follows closely the

(Third preceding page) The Clearwater River flows swift and shallow through the Black Canyon area.

(Second preceding page) Fireweed adorns the slopes of Deer Ridge in the Kaniksu National Forest.

(Preceding page, above) Mist creeps along the shore of Little Redfish Lake, where sparkling reflections provide a mirror image of the rugged Sawtooth Range.

(Preceding page, below) Old Hyndman Peak is a lone rocky spur rising from the Pioneer Mountains.

(Left) This view of the jagged Sawtooth Range, from Little Redfish Lake, makes the mountain's name seem particularly apt.

(Following page) The colors of autumn glow along this peaceful stretch of the Salmon River.

(Second following page, above) North Idaho's lake country spreads in a panorama below this solitary skier.

(Second following page, below) Springtime touches the fertile Idaho farm country with green.

(Preceding pages) Stanley Lake offers a rippling reflection of McGowan Peak, high in the Sawtooth Range.
(Left) A portion of the Lochsa River's course is through peaceful forest country like this.
(Below) Ice pressure ridges break the smooth frozen surface of Bear Lake.
(Opposite) A brilliant rainbow arches over the open landscape near Lewiston.
(Following page) Another rainbow climbs through the mist of Upper Mesa Falls, on Henrys Fork of the Snake River.

(Preceding page, above) Lush pastureland provides forage for these Idaho beef cattle.

(Preceding page, below) The touch of early autumn can be seen in this quiet backwater of Pend Oreille Lake, near Sandpoint.

(Opposite) Fourth of July Lake sparkles from high in the White Cloud Range, in the Challis National Forest.

(Right) A solitary pine graces this garden on the shore of Hayden Lake.

(Below) Trackless snow ornaments this deserted barn and corrral north of Soda Springs.

(Following page, above) Shrunken by summer's heat, this Idaho river gives over part of its rocky bed to tall grasses.

(Following page, below) Wild rose hips add a touch of color to the late-summer aspect of Nez Perce County wheatfields.

intricate profile of its eastern shoreline. Coeur d'Alene is regarded by the raters and classifiers as Number 5 among the most beautiful lakes in the world. That's right up there, but probably a bit conservative. It's difficult to imagine anything to surpass the transcendent loveliness of Beauty Bay. Forested hills drop down to the water's edge, enfolding the lake in a series of coves that seem to pull the visitor into a timeless zone of great peace.

Coeur d'Alene Lake became a "magnificent millpond" toward the end of the 19th century when sawmills formed the nucleus of the town of Coeur d'Alene on the lake's northern shore. The vast white-pine forests of the St. Joe, Coeur d'Alene, and St. Maries River valleys supplied the raw product, which was floated down the Coeur d'Alene and St. Joe Rivers. Coeur d'Alene grew so fast it was incorporated as a city in 1907. Its growth had been spurred by the Northern Pacific Railroad, built through the wild Northwest in 1881-83. The ferocious cost of building the rail line may have been the goad that moved company officials to embellish the news of a gold strike in the Coeur d' Alene Mountains in 1883. Their propaganda was at least partly responsible for the frantic surge of thousands of miners into Spokane and Rathdrum by train and finally into Coeur d'Alene, the "base camp," by stage. The town grew and the railroad prospered.

Among Idaho's wealth of river systems, none is more esteemed for its placid beauty than the St. Joe River. The St. Joe is the antithesis of all the usual white-water streams. Their take-charge pace lets you know you'd better pay attention. But the "shadowy St. Joe" is a slow, meandering, friendly sort for the greater part of its 125 miles. After a hurried beginning in the high glacial creeks and lakes of the Bitterroot Mountains, it becomes peaceful, calm, dignified. Flowing through the wide, green meadows of its valley, the St. Joe becomes quiet and deep. The lack of falls or rapids on the lower river makes it an ideal "working" stream. It is still used to float logs to Lake Coeur d'Alene and its sawmills.

The extraordinary beauty of the St. Joe River and its countryside began to draw settlers not long after Lake Coeur d'Alene was discovered. The willows and cottonwoods lining its banks are mirrored in its green waters, giving it the "shadowy" moniker. After settlers discovered the St. Joe, so did vacationers, many from far-away places. The river became known as the best trout stream in the country and for awhile was heavily exploited for that fish, even to the extent of dynamiting by commercial fishermen. All but sport fishing is now banned on Idaho's streams, and the St. Joe is still a very good fishing stream, especially its North Fork. Today there

(Preceding page) The rocky bed of the Salmon River provides its surface with frequent ripples and whitewater.

are camp sites along the river where the magnificent river and its lush valley may be appreciated at first hand. The St. Joe is unusual even to the end of its course, where it flows into Lake Coeur d' Alene. There it has built up its own channel through the eastern end of the lake by depositing banks of silt, now overgrown with vegetation. It flows between these islands at its own pace, although the lake waters are all around.

The St. Joe is the highest navigable river in the world. Boats can travel it to 2,198 feet above sea level. In the "nobody's perfect" category, the St. Joe sometimes does something a bit excessive. It floods. But in this imperfect world beauty always has its dark side.

Up where the Panhandle becomes a 40-mile-wide corridor with east and west borders following perfectly straight political lines, is Idaho's biggest lake—Pend Oreille. The French names of this and other Idaho lakes and towns are a legacy of the French-Canadian trappers who traded with the Indians in the area. Coeur d' Alene, meaning roughly "the sharp pointed heart," was the label they tacked onto an Indian tribe who were very sharp traders. Lake Pend Oreille is named for the Pend d' Oreille Indians who lived in the region of the big lake.

Still farther north, quite remote in its corner of the Panhandle, is Priest Lake. For all its lush, forested neighborhood it is conveniently near Spokane, that outsized eastern Washington community. The folks there consider Priest and the other Panhandle lakes their very own summer playgrounds. Upper Priest Lake is still preserved as a semi-wilderness, reached by boat from the lower lake.

The measure of what is good in this life is not always in how much of it there is. The gentle jumble of mountains, rivers, lakes, meadowlands, and valleys called the Panhandle is squeezed into a very small space. So far it has escaped any major exploitative projects, except for the extractive ones. But mining is no longer done on a confiscatory scale, and lumbering is on a sustaining basis. The environmental concern shown by present-day northern Idahoans is a good indication that the Panhandle's unique beauty will be available far into the future for wild creatures to live in and for human creatures to appreciate.

(Following page) The Snake River makes its way through harsh and rugged country in the south of Idaho, breaking into several cataracts at Shoshone Falls, near Twin Falls.

Northern and Central Idaho

Just south of the Panhandle it's still northern Idaho: the state has a north that covers a lot of territory. South of the Panhandle the countryside begins to have a different appearance. Between St. Maries and Grangeville, some 150 miles by road, the skies and the land open up into vistas of vast fertile grainfields under a blue canopy. Near Lewiston, where the Snake River veers west into Washington, orchards are part of the scene. The region makes moderate use of irrigating systems because these valley lands receive less moisture than the Panhandle country.

Idaho's north-south highway, US 95, follows the extreme western side as far south as Lewiston. Then it turns southeast through the Nez Perce Indian Reservation to Grangeville. A few miles farther is White Bird Hill, one of Idaho's premier viewpoints. White Bird overlooks scenery done up in the grand style. The wild Salmon River can be seen dashing up from the south and turning west for its rendezvous with the Snake. Deep gorges crowd the panorama. Stretching east, west, and south, they transfix the observer as symbols of the river's immense power. Off on the blue-purple southwest horizon a great mountain wall can be seen: the high and rugged Seven Devils Mountains that line up on the Idaho side of Hells Canyon. At Grangeville itself, to back up a few miles, a more gentle prospect opens up. The highway eases down a long, rolling hill and enters a meadowland whose soft beauty has mesmerized many a traveler: 30-mile-long Camas Prairie. Here the Indians used to dig the camas root, but now waves of golden wheat cover rolling hills.

The Nez Perce Reservation lies to the north, between Lewiston and Orofino. The Nez Perce National Historical Park is located here and in the White Bird Battlefield area, illustrating the history and customs of the Nez Perce. The tribal saga includes the tragic events of 1877, when Chief Joseph, while fighting off the U.S. Army, conducted his masterly retreat toward Canada from the Indian ancestral lands in the Wallowas. To commemorate this retreat, every year riders on spotted Appaloosa horses—the breed raised by the Nez Perce for mountain travel—trace 100 miles of the Lolo Trail, a part of the 1,300-mile route of the Nez Perce march.

(Preceding page, above) The old Lolo Trail was the route of the Lewis and Clark Expedition, and this view of Green Saddle may be the same scene explorers saw.
(Preceding page, below) Ghostlike, snow-laden pines stand on the drifted slopes of the Schweitzer Ski Area in the Selkirk Mountains.

The auto traveler can follow the Lolo Trail today on US 12, which follows closely the route of Lewis and Clark. The road enters Idaho at Lolo Pass, cuts through the lofty Bitterroot Range along the banks of the Lochsa River, then meets the Selway River to become the Middle Fork of the Clearwater. At the confluence of the Middle and South Fork, it becomes the main Clearwater, veering north and west to Lewiston and eventually the Snake. This course traverses some of the finest mountain country in all of Idaho. Those who like their traveling on the scary side may navigate rubber boats from Moose Creek to Selway Falls on the Selway River, a white-water odyssey that is reserved for the very brave.

A town with a beautiful Spanish name—Orofino—is the gateway to northern Idaho's spectacular mountains and forests, including the Selway-Bitterroot Wilderness. Orofino is itself built into a canyon breached only by the Clearwater River and the highway. The name suggests Orofino's gold mining past; it is in fact still a mining town. But its primary livelihood now is lumber. That's not very surprising—the most densely timbered mountains in the state surround it. State Highway 11 from Orofino goes back into the mountainous environs where the prospectors of the 1860s endured a harsh existence in the hope of finding yellow treasure.

The area is richly endowed with splashing mountain streams and forested, rolling ridges. If you look around from the top of one of these mountains the ridges seem to go on forever. The town of Elk River, across Dworshak Reservoir from Orofino, features, nearby, one of the area's beautiful spectacles. Elk Creek, on its way to the reservoir, roars over a stairstep series of falls 200 feet high, with one straight plunge of 110 feet. This is all Indian country, or course. Many of the topographical features, such as rock formations, had specific meanings and roles in Indian mythology. Historical markers along US 12 recall the times before the white man's intrusion and help to recreate the Indian presence by reminding us that this land was a living entity to the Nez Perce and other tribes who lived here.

When the traveler heads for Lewiston from any other point in Idaho his vertical direction is always down. The lumber town at the confluence of the Clearwater and the Snake is, after all, the lowest point in the state: alt. 738 feet. Like many Idaho towns, it is cupped within a ring of hills that rise around it like protecting walls. They help to shield Lewiston from most weather extremes; "banana belt" is the expression sometimes applied to the area, though you may have to take that with a little salt.

(Left) Greenery above ground testifies to the presence of water in this desert wash at Craters of the Moon National Monument.

The great natural *force majeur* of central Idaho is that mighty and violent river, the Salmon. For size and brute strength it rivals the Snake itself. For pure drama it has no peer. Fed by countless tributaries that have their origins in the glaciers, lakes, and springs of the great mass of central Idaho mountains, the Salmon reaches west across the waist of Idaho, in effect cutting the state in half. It is wholly an Idaho river, 425 miles long, one of the longest rivers that begin and end in the same state. Other statistics about it are impressive, too. It flows in all four directions from the Sawtooth Wilderness Area, draining four national forests, including the Idaho Primitive Area. After doing all these things it finally bequeaths its waters to the Snake where that river forms the border with the Wallowa country of Oregon.

Central Idaho's Sawtooth Mountains, where things begin for the Salmon, have been given status as a national recreation and wilderness area. Whatever their official designation, this mighty cluster of jumbled ridges and sharp peaks still guard some sheltered valleys and cold, clear streams where no human foot has ever trod and no human fisherman has ever cast a line. Stanley Basin is not one of these places. Being one of the few parts of Sawtooth Valley accessible by road, it is very popular with Idahoans for its high mountain meadows and alpine lakes of extraordinary beauty. The lakes are the result of glacial carving and of course are situated at high elevations—around 6,000 feet—walled in by fierce peaks of the Sawtooths reaching in the 10,000-foot range. The basin is a giant pastureland, too, where in summer great flocks of sheep and herds of cattle graze on the lush grass. The half-round wagons of the Basque sheepherders are still sometimes a part of the picture in the Sawtooth Valley.

The mountain kingdom of the Sawtooths is quite gentle, for all its rugged wilderness demeanor. That is not to say it's a pushover for any novice explorer who sees its peaks as an easy challenge (they're not, say those who know). But its forests are friendly and offer exceptional opportunities in the autumn months for hikers who find nature at her most bewitching when frosty nights etch the leaves in dazzling colors. The long Sawtooth Valley makes it easy for the novice outdoorsman to get around without losing himself among the trees and lakes and creeks. Indian summer in the Sawtooths may last through October, and the warm days and crisp nights are especially delightful when, as sometimes happens, Pacific zephyrs waft through the wilderness, spreading the fresh aromas of pine and fir over the foothills and valleys.

It is possible to see a great deal of this country at one magnificent viewpoint that rises in its midst. This is Galena Summit, an 8,701-foot perch in the southern part of the range, south of Obsidian on US 93. To the west, the Sawtooths cut sharply into the sky like jagged razor blades; the eastern sky is punctuated by the aptly-named White Cloud Peaks, with summits well over 10,000 feet. Some idea of central Idaho's amazing profusion of mountain ranges—there are more than 80—is possible for the observer at Galena Summit as he scans the crowded panorama.

The Salmon River and its several forks are omnipresent in central Idaho. The Middle Fork of the Salmon is considered one of the most hair-raising challenges to white-water runners. It is indeed the epitome of the headlong parent stream, rising in the higher reaches of the Sawtooths like the main river it eventually joins. The Middle Fork seems to attract the eminent and notorious for vacation adventure, including presidents and potentates.

The Salmon's dominance extends into the huge Idaho Primitive Area; the Middle Fork rushes north through the eastern part of the region's one million acres. Although not yet designated wilderness, the Primitive Area can out-wilderness other preserves that already have the label. Parts of six Idaho national forests have dense stands of timber on the slopes of its lofty mountains. Game roams free and unobserved through its canyons and along its pure, icy streams, where the aroma of pine and fir cleanses the spirit of those few persons who found their way into its secret places. Many millenia ago the ancestors of the Shoshone are believed to have lived here, or at least to have visited its deep canyons on hunting forays.

The 60-mile-long Primitive Area ends at the main Salmon River, which bounds it on the north, but it really continues on north of the river as the Salmon River Breaks Primitive Area. This parcel lies for 40 miles along the north bank of the big river, 217,185 acres of wild country that few people have ever seen, except from the air or from boats. The primitive areas are open to hunters and fishermen, but lack of roads keeps the numbers down. The mule deer is far more numerous here than any other animal, the rest being in the seldom-seen category. Mountain goats and bighorn sheep frequent the high and inaccessible places, preferring not to reveal their whereabouts to anybody at all, be he bear, moose, cougar, or person.

A corridor of unprotected land on the north separates these preserves from the vast Selway-Bitterroot Wilderness that lies along the eastern border and encompasses the Bitterroot Mountains. Its western reach takes in the upper Selway River drainage. If all of these preserves were joined together into one gigantic wilderness, as conservationists hope, the resulting three-and-one-half million acres would be the biggest such preserve in the country outside of Alaska.

(Following page) Paintbrush and Gentian bloom in this meadow at the foot of the peaks of the White Cloud Range.

The wild country, so labeled, is only a small part of central Idaho's great expanse of territory that is just as rugged and, so far, pretty much unspoiled. There are, to be sure, towns in some of the river valleys and mountain canyons, but their presence is more an assurance than an intrusion. Towns like Arco and Challis in east-central Idaho are small-scale settlements that fit into the big-mountain country in a symbiotic way. For the nature-lover and searcher after scenic *chefs-d'oeuvre*, the towns serve as reference and access points from which to observe the mystic beauties fashioned by the changing light of day upon the mountainous folds that crowd the horizon.

All of this is a rather round-about buildup to a picture that is available to any traveler on US 93 between Challis and Salmon, or on Alt. 93 southeast from Challis toward Arco. The up-and-down wilderness that characterizes much of Idaho seems to come together in this corner of the state, dominated as it is by three great mountain systems. The most massive grouping of all Idaho's mountains, the Salmon River system is here. They run from about Stanley northeast to the border, rising from the Salmon River itself. Two parallel ranges, Lost River and Lemhi, stretch away to the southeast.

The town of Challis is perhaps a good anchor point for a trip through these mountain fastnesses; a drive north to Salmon or south to Arco is a journey through a fantasy landscape where color and form together provide a visual and emotional experience that may be unavailable in quite the same intensity anywhere else. Merely to be in Challis itself is reason enough for rejoicing. It and Salmon City have been placed in extraordinarily beautiful settings, although Challis may have the edge. The Salmon River Mountains to the northeast exude a certain picturesque aura that is observable whatever the time of day. But there is a best time, and that is at sunset, with one's visual receptors pointed away from Salmon toward Challis. With this orientation, the sun itself, weather permitting, takes center stage, loafing around in the western sky where the near and far mountains, perhaps along with some strategically placed clouds, display marvelous ranges and intensities of color. The bluffs by the river may be bathed in irridescent mist. Distant peaks glitter like polished gold. Low cloud layers at mid-height seem to pulse with interior fire as they catch the slanting rays of the sun.

The journey from Arco along the Lost River valley may be less massively theatrical than the Challis-Salmon stretch, but it has its moments. The mountains plump up in denuded brown hills that sit on great, rugged bases. Mount Borah, the highest point in Idaho (12,662), commands respect not only for size but for the ample

(Preceding page) Sawtooth Lake lies high among the peaks of the Sawtooth Range.

lines of its great treeless torso. The Lost River system, though stark by some standards, reveals a sunlit loveliness that is all the more remarkable for the almost complete absence of trees.

The special quality of the Lost River spur and the Lemhi range to the east of it is also found in the town of Arco itself. In its alpine setting more than a mile up it looks like a postcard mountain town. Being on a bend in the river doesn't hurt either. The Lost River Range ends at this point in Wildcat Peak, which is the town's backdrop. Small wonder that the Mormons came up from Utah (in 1855) to establish an agricultural colony in the Lemhi valley. They would have made it, too, if they hadn't been evicted by the Indians three years later. But they named the beautiful area after Limhi (sic), a personage in the Book of Mormon. Now, although the remains of their old fort are all that is left from their stay, their early settlement is remembered in the name Lemhi, now applied to a valley, mountain range, river, forest, and even county.

(Following page, above) Mt. Borah, at 12,665 feet the highest peak in Idaho, lies in the Lost River Range.
(Following page, below) Trees of the Nez Perce National Forest seem inverted in the still waters of Seven Devils Lake.

(Third preceding page) Plumes of bear grass are familiar sights in Idaho mountain meadows.

(Second preceding page) Gaunt and lifeless tree trunks stand like sentinels over the pines that grow below Big Fog Mountain in the Selway-Bitterroot Wilderness.

(Preceding page, above) Peaks tower over Hells Canyon, keeping the Snake River in shadow except at midday.

(Preceding page, below) Beauty Bay is an arm of Lake Coeur d' Alene, seen here from Mineral Ridge.

(Left) The peaceful waters of Lucky Peak Reservoir repose under the rimrock of Idaho's bare hills.

(Following page) Tenacious wildflowers find a toehold in one of the Frozen Rivers of Lava, at Craters of the Moon National Monument.

(Second following page, above) Rocky bluffs tower behind this peaceful bend in the Coeur d' Alene River, above Eneville.

(Second following page, below) Vegetation crowds close to the Snake River in the barren country east of Idaho Falls.

(Left) Glistening coldly in the sunshine of early spring, the waters of Sawtooth Lake seem to remind the viewer of their snowy origin. Mt. Regan towers in the background.

(Preceding pages) Glistening coldly in the sunshine of early spring, the waters of Sawtooth Lake seem to remind the viewer of their snowy origin. Mt. Regan towers in the background.

(Left) Cool evening breezes bring out colorful sailboats on the sun-dappled waters of Lake Coeur d' Alene.

(Below) A few aquatic plants grace the shores in the Island Park Reservoir in the bare reaches of eastern Idaho.

(Opposite) Peaks of the White Cloud Range rise sharply behind Phyllis Lake, in the Challis National Forest.

(Following page) Mossy rocks add to the greenness in the well-watered Salmon River Canyon.

(Preceding page, above) It's a long way down for a drink of water in Bruneau Canyon.

(Preceding page, below) Spatter cones are among the weird volcanic phenomena visible at Craters of the Moon National Monument.

(Opposite) This lovely stretch of the main Salmon River is being considered for wilderness designation by the Federal Government.

(Right) Ocean spray blooms on Wood Rat Hill, above the waters of Priest Lake.

(Below) Colorful flowers bloom at the summit of White Bird Hill, looking toward the Salmon River Canyon.

(Following page, above) Late afternoon sun adds a reddish glow to the stark gauntness of the Seven Devils Mountains, seen here from Heaven's Gate.

(Following page, below) Autumn's gold has begun to touch the trees along the banks of the Salmon River.

THE KINGDOM OF THE SNAKE

The River

Idaho is a big state. One need not make any wild surmises to observe this on a map. The slender northern panhandle is like the iceberg's tip—the base is a long way down and there's a lot more to it. The "fat" part of Idaho, in the south, is the home of the legendary life-giving Snake River. The wide Snake River Plain, so different from the northern areas, is another country in all but name.

The Snake River is a very long drink of water. It wanders 1,036 miles across the West, from the southeastern part of Yellowstone Park to its meeting with the Columbia River near Pasco, in the Palouse Hills of eastern Washington. By far the longest part of the river's journey is through eastern, south-central, and western Idaho. The Snake veers northwest for some 60 miles after it crosses the border, then begins a long southwest arc across the lava plains of Idaho. For more than 300 miles the river flows across this wide plain, dropping more then 3,000 feet by the time it gets to the western border. It is a magnificent stream where it has been allowed to flow freely. Some testimony to this is the deep, narrow gorge it has cut along much of its course. The river's drop gets even steeper when it turns north to form a part of the western border. Here the Snake has cut the deepest of all gorges, Hells Canyon. In this 80-mile stretch the drop is 600 feet and the rapids immensely powerful. Downstream from the canyon the big river receives the waters of two only slightly lesser streams—the Salmon and the Clearwater. Thus swollen, it turns to the northwest at Lewiston for its final rush to the Columbia.

The Southeast

Eastern Idaho is a variety of things, some of them down-right strange. The edge of the desert-like Snake River Plain is here, but so also are mountains and forests and tributary streams of the Snake. The tributaries come in mostly from the south and east, where the mountains are. North of the Plain, many rivers flowing toward the Snake do so underground, having dropped their waters through the porous

(Preceding page) Snow completely covers these mountain pines in Bonner Country's Schweitzer Basin Ski area.

volcanic rock. The northeast corner is high mountain country with flashing streams, crystal lakes, and the big Targhee National Forest, haunt of moose and elk, bear and deer. Yet slightly to the west of the mountain town of St. Anthony, and reaching 30 miles north and south, are the Scenic Sand Dunes, a most curious phenomenon. The dunes not only seem to have wandered from their proper location by a sea somewhere; they also have the remarkable ability to take on the hues of the evening sky when the sun is at its orange-red best.

St. Anthony is on Henry's Fork of the Snake River. Henry's Fork is noteworthy for at least two reasons. North of the town, the stream has two close-together falls of unusual height and beauty. Upper and Lower Mesa Falls are made to order for waterfall watchers. Way up in the northeast corner (another ten miles or so) is a high mountain lake for which Idahoans and others claim the world's best trout fishing. All of this is easily approachable on US 20 from Ashton. Southeast of Ashton, state routes 32 and 33 run parallel to the gorgeous Teton range, which lines up on the border of Idaho and Wyoming. These roads give the auto tourist a close view, from the west, of the theatrical Teton spires.

Boise, Idaho's biggest city, is over in the west, but eastern Idaho has the two next in size—Pocatello and Idaho Falls. These communities are big enough to be important without submerging vast stretches of surrounding terrain under the paraphernalia of urban society. Idaho Falls, a good-looking town, is, as its name implies, the site of one of the Snake River's monumental cataracts. The falls is not high, but stretches across the river in a great arc 1,500 feet wide, with beauty both visual and auditory. The sound of the tumbling, foaming waters is heard throughout the city, a constant accompaniment to the daily life there.

Farther along the southwestward-swinging arc of the upper Snake is Pocatello, Idaho's big processing and shipping center. Along with Blackfoot and Idaho Falls, Pocatello receives the bountiful harvest made possible by the extensive irrigation projects that have turned the desert-like Snake River Plain into a "Magic Valley." Bringing water to thirsty plant roots has made southern Idaho one of the world's most productive agricultural regions. The fertile soil, long growing season, lots of sunshine, and lack of violent storms, such as the tornadoes common to the Midwest, add up to plentiful crops of highly nutrituous vegetables. The Idaho potato is still the *piece de resistance* on gourmet tables where the elite meet to eat. The region's history is distinctly Mormon, with some French-Canadian mixed in. Trappers from the north were among the earliest white men to venture into the area. They left their mark on

(Following page) Slender, white-trunked birches cast wintry shadows on the snow near Diamond Creek, northwest of Soda Springs.

at least one town near the Utah border, a town still very much alive although its name might discourage longevity. For some reason the beaver trappers started calling it Malade (now Malad) City. The French-Canadians supposedly got sick so often when they were in town they decided to give the place a name to fit the occasion. Their illness has been variously attributed to drinking the water of the Malad River, stuffing themselves on beaver meat, or ingesting bad booze. No one really knows.

The Mormon influence is pervasive in this pocket southeast of the Snake. Franklin, the oldest town (1860) and a hair's breadth from the border, was started by Mormons, and so was Montpelier (1863), close to the corner on US 89 where it intersects US 30. The Caribou National Forest covers much of this region, where the previously noted phosphates are so plentiful. Mineral springs are also plentiful, and the economies of some high mountain towns, like Soda Springs and Lava Hot Springs, are linked closely to their role as health spas.

Idaho's share of Bear Lake is only half a lake. The other half is in Utah. But Bear Lake, whatever state it's in, makes a positive contribution to the physical environment. It is big—20 miles long, eight wide, and about 200 feet deep. Enfolded within the hills of southeastern Idaho and northeastern Utah, it is a popular recreational lake for people with disparate ideas on what the outdoors are there for. In midsummer its surface temperature is ideal for swimming. Varieties of trout lurk in the cooler depths. In winter, when the lake waters turn to polar bear temperatures and the lake winds follow suit, swimming loses its appeal, but a form of fishing takes place over a short time span in January. For a two-week period a spawning run of whitefish occurs, and the more weatherproof members of the fishing fraternity go after them with nets.

The South-Central Plain

Idaho has been taking its own sweet time in allowing itself to be discovered by the touring public. Some unredeemed wilderness lovers, however, have long been aware of the hidden riches behind the sagebrush-and-desert label pinned on this land for so long by the casual tourists who knew little more than the land on either side of US 30. As the world's wilderness shrinks, interest in the state and what it has to offer is on the increase. The Snake River Plain is getting its share of attention.

The steppe-like plains country probably will never become a tourist draw in the Yellowstone or Yosemite sense. For one thing, roads into it are bound to remain scarce, because building them over the tortuous, volcanic terrain is almost

(Preceding page) The rising sun casts this brilliant reflection on the dark waters of a mountain tarn, for the eyes of early risers only.

impossible, except at great expense. But even the timeless geology of this sere land has been altered in recent years by man's amazing ability to shape his environment. Irrigation is changing ways of life on the dry plateau, making the fertile soil bloom with agricultural riches. The river has been tamed by reclamation dams—like Palisades, American Falls, and Minidoka. Some say it's a grievous price to pay for farming the desert. But the people who thought up the term "Magic Valley" for these irrigated lands obviously don't think so.

If the enormous Idaho aquifer could be tapped on a larger scale maybe the water-storage dams wouldn't be so crucial. The aquifer is an immense subterranean reservoir built up by rainfall and by streams from the northern mountains, such as Big Lost River, which disappears into a lava formation. Water sinks into the porous volcanic layer of the plateau and is stored underground, much of it eventually reaching the Snake through seepage and underground channels. If you look at a map of this plain you will see few tributaries coming in from the north, but the Snake eventually receives their waters—under the table, so to speak.

As we have seen, the Snake rules a kingdom that has more than its share of odd phenomena, features that seem to epitomize the strangeness of the environment. The Crystal Ice Caves are an example. The caves, a recent discovery 15 miles northwest of American Falls, contain an ocean of underground ice and feature icy stalactites and stalagmites that on occasion resemble sculptured figures. The caves are a cool oasis during the relentless summer heat of the plains. The caverns of ice were created by a fissure in the lava overlay, now memorialized as the Great Rift National Landmark.

Craters of the Moon National Monument is a more well-known oddity about 33 air miles off to the northwest on the northern edge of the Plain, not far from Arco. Here the mountains begin to assert themselves, and the area is generally higher than the southern part of the Plain. The big (83 square miles) Craters region is one of the most desolate places imaginable on earth. Its resemblance to a moonscape is startling. But its desolation is not uniform or monotonous. There are flat fields of fresh-looking lava and cindery craters and buttes of various shapes and heights. The lava is mostly pure black but sometimes occurs in variations of red and rust. For those whose curiosity requires a more detailed look, there's a seven-mile paved loop that passes close to some of the grotesque formations and over the fields of cinders. Trails from the road allow further exploration of the area, riddled as it is with tunnels and caves. Off the trails, walking is extremely chancey unless the walker has some lava-proof footwear. There are a great many ice caves in southern Idaho, and Craters of the

(Left) Boundary County's scenery tends toward rugged mountains and lakes in the northernmost portion of Idaho.

Moon has some of them. It also has some plant life, like the limber pine, testifying to the tenacity of life forms on this planet.

Meanwhile, the Snake has been rolling along, and 75 miles directly south of Sun Valley it has reached Twin Falls, the biggest town of the south-central plain. On the way south through the barren plains is yet another underground ice cavern, the Shoshone Ice Caves, with a variety of chambers and formations. These caves, being easier to reach than some of the other ice caverns, are probably the best known of them all. Just down the road is Shoshone itself, a tree-shaded oasis that offers a cool refuge in summer from the fierce heat of the plains that surround it. The town is architecturally in tune with the land. The construction material in many cases has been the porous lava rock that is so abundantly available here.

These strange landscapes possess an intense kind of beauty that strikes at one's deepest emotions when he becomes absorbed in them and by them. Fittingly, the Snake has carved itself some gorgeous palisades here, conveniently observable north of Twin Falls from a human artifact that fits beautifully into the spare and powerful panorama—a cantilever bridge high above the river. Downriver about 20 miles one of those streams from the faraway northeast (so the theory goes) that didn't make it to the Snake in the traditional manner of tributaries, gives up its substance in spectacular fashion at Thousand Springs. Water from this so-called lost river splashes and sprays out of the cliffside east of Hagerman in joyful abandon, as if glad to have escaped from its underground prison.

Reaching the southwestern corner of Idaho, the Snake begins a long, slow swing to the north that doesn't really make a definite commitment to that direction until the border is reached. The Snake River Plain is left behind; with irrigation, much of that fertile land has been made to bloom. But irrigation won't do much for the harsh, eroded Owyhee desert that accounts for most of the land southwest of the river's big bend. This piece of wasteland is like still another country from the Snake River Plain, a dead land that seems alien to the planet earth. From the human point of view perhaps it is, except for a small mountainous patch in the northwestern corner. There are a half-dozen or so towns in this soul-searing country huddled for the most part by or near the Snake, as if to get very far away would doom them to a fiery plunge into the pitiless, devastated lands to the south. The towns contain nearly all the population of Owyhee County: around 6,500.

There's an awful lot of the Owyhee desert that has never felt the imprint of a human foot, shod or not, or of a tire tread, either. In the mountainous northern regions of Idaho east-west roads are scarce; in the desolate Owyhee country almost no paved roads at all can be found. It's just hard to put them on sand dunes or over ravaged landscapes that often depart from the horizontal into scary, deep canyons, like the one cut by the Bruneau River on its way north to the Snake. Bruneau Canyon is more then 60 winding miles long, and in some places its sheer, narrow gorge slices 2,000 feet into the plateau. To get a drink of water in this desert you have to go where it is—probably more than 1,000 feet straight down a basaltic cleft in the earth.

But some of the local residents are not terribly concerned about a lack of roads or with having to live in a rough neighborhood. These particular residents are birds of prey and they ride the wind currents that are constantly present in the Snake River canyon that borders the Owyhee country on the north. On and above some 31 miles of land along the river, designated the Snake River Birds of Prey Natural Area (BPNA), live more raptors per acre than anywhere else in the world.

The BPNA covers about 26,000 acres of habitat especially suited to birds of prey. The big birds—the golden eagles and the great horned owls—need the updrafts for lift. But the smaller hunters—the hawks, falcons and kestrels—ride them too. The riverside cliffs provide plenty of the rocky and inaccessible nesting spots these birds require, and the dry countryside teems with prey: reptiles, mice, squirrels, rabbits and smaller birds. Because they've been left alone, predator and prey live in natural balance, regulating each other by a primal law of supply and demand. This-out-of-the way area provides one other essential benefit to its beaked-and-taloned residents: pesticides, passed up through the food chain, endanger the birds' reproduction by reducing the thickness of their fragile eggshells. In this remote, "unimproved," sun-tortured wilderness, pesticide concentrations are still tolerably low. Preservationists hope to get more land on both sides of the big river added to the raptors' refuge, but agricultural interests are fighting such a move.

There is something essentially grand and awesome about birds that eat fresh meat: these airborne hunters have earned the respect—and sometimes fear—of mankind through all ages. Size is one factor. The golden eagle, with its seven-foot wingspan, is among the biggest animals you'll find in the air, and even the smaller raptors are big for birds. But more than size, there is an admiration for an animal beautifully adapted to a difficult task. Humankind are physically generalist, capable of doing a variety of things adequately, if not magnificently, given the appropriate tools. But man's dexterity pales in grandeur beside the form of an animal which does one thing very well, and it is no wonder that the fine-honed grace and purposeful

(Following page) Centuries of erosion have created this unusual sight: Balanced Rock, near Twin Falls.

economy in the appearance of a hawk, owl, or eagle, and their unimpeachable wildness, can generate awe and respect. Even our language reflects our feelings for these sharp-eyed hunters: we may refer to something as "bird-brained," or use a variety of epithets related to poultry, but for the raptors there is nothing but praise: "eyes like a hawk," "proud as an eagle," or "wise as an owl." Their only enemy is man.

The Deepest Canyon

At the western limits of southern Idaho the Snake curls gradually around the corner of the state and heads due north—with a wriggle here and there—for a run through the deep gorges of the western border, culminating in the most colossal cut of all—Hells Canyon. The pace of the Snake steps up as the descent gets steeper; the river sweeps unchained past the population centers of the southwest corner, as careless of them as it was of the Indian villages that once were clustered on its banks. It seems to be in a hurry to come down from the high southern desert for a joyous, furious plunge through the outside trench it has dug on Idaho's western flank.

Three times the Snake is interrupted in its wild dash. Downstream from the confluence of the Powder River, Brownlee Dam raises a low profile over a river that has become, for the moment, a lake of quiet water—a reservoir. But the impetuous Snake surges through the penstocks of the dam on to yet another concrete wall—Oxbow—a few miles downstream. Finally, after butting against dam number three—Hells Canyon—at the very head of the canyon itself, the river reverts to form and goes crashing in soaring waves and wild rapids through the canyon. On the Idaho side, the summit of He Devil Peak towers an awesome 8,000 feet or more above the river. Released from its temporary imprisonment, the Snake seems bent on making up for that humiliation. It still takes a large portion of nerve to ride the river in one of those big inflatable rafts. Giant waves and curls can suck in the rafts, flip them over, and spit them out with never an apology for the inconvenience and threat to life and limb. Now big jet boats bull their way against the powerful current—about the only fairly certain way to ride the river intact and unsoaked.

The river boils and surges in shadows at the bottom of the gorge, narrow and dark and deep. Above it basalt cliffs rise as much as 2,000 feet, and above them the mountains slope away, treeless and covered with grass. Unlike the Grand Canyon where the sensation of great depths is immediate, in this gorge the shoulders of the

(Preceding page) This view from Dry Diggins Lookout tends to explain the unusual name as the barren landscape stretches off in every direction.

mountains generally block the view of their peaks. It is only occasionally, upon rounding a bend or grabbing a glimpse of a distant peak, that the traveler gets the full sense of the canyon's depth.

Ancient Indians dwelt at the canyon bottom beside the furious water during winters, because the climate at river level is much milder than that of the mountains above. There are about 200 archaeological sites in the unflooded portion of the canyon: subtle pictographs in ochre on the overhanging cliffs, and occasional brushy depressions where lodges may once have stood. But in spite of the sense of timelessness one can feel among these faint remnants of another civilization, people who know the canyon say it is changing. The dams upstream hijack the loads of sediment that once formed natural beaches, and in the wild portion of the canyon sand deposits are simply washing away.

Today Hells Canyon is endangered equally but differently from two sides. One side, apparently indifferent to the wild and free river, or putting other concerns in higher priority, would like to see at least one more dam, silencing another 50 miles or so of the river's roar. So far, conservationists have managed to prevent further dam construction. But the river is also in danger from the people who love it: its fragile ecology cannot bear the burden of the increasing numbers of tourists who come to run its rapids and camp on its banks.

(Following page) Sunset turns the peaceful surface of the Pend Oreille River to a rosy-golden hue.